Table of content

1. A brief Intro...........................page2
2. Wise men's view......................page3

A BRIFE INTRO

I am a young man with quest for real value. I've lived with the rich and with the poor, with the old and with the young, with the both the male figure as well as the female figure, and I have also seen them all in their financially "big time" and their "small times" ...

I have seen them speak and I looked upon their books and journals, I have asked them question and have also been silent with them.

Watching and studying these men, I offer to share with you some of the rarest things financially successful people will ever say to you.

Sit tight and enjoy this write-up as it will surely be a guide and equally a motivator to get up and smash your financial goals.

Financial stability, to me is being at a state of financial rest. Being able to foot your bills without much taught.

Let us talk finance it the pages of this book.

WISE MEN'S VIEW ON FINANCE

1. "Money is better than poverty, if only for financial reasons." – Woody Allen

2. "It is incumbent upon each of us to improve spending and savings practices to ensure our own individual financial security and preserve the collective economic well-being of our great society." – Ron Lewis

3. "The goal isn't more money. The goal is living life on your terms." – Will Rogers

4. "If you're not staying on top of your money, you're putting your financial well-being at risk." – Suze Orman

5. "I have enough money to last me the rest of my life, unless I buy something." – Jackie Mason

6. "If we command our wealth, we shall be rich and free. If our wealth commands us, we are poor indeed." – Edmund Burke p l

7. "Financial freedom is available to those who learn about it and work for it." – Robert Kiyosaki

8. "Wealth is the ability to fully experience life." – Henry David Thoreau

9. "Financial peace isn't the acquisition of stuff. It's learning to live on less than you make, so you can give money back and have money to invest. You can't win until you do this." – Dave Ramsey

10. "Money is a terrible master but an excellent servant." – P.T. Barnum

11. "You must gain control over your money or the lack of it will forever control you." – Dave Ramsey

12. "Have a well-thought financial plan that is not dependent upon correctly guessing what will happen in the future." – Barry Ritholtz

13. "Do what you love and the money will follow." – Marsha Sinetar

14. "Pursuing your passion is fulfilling and leads to financial freedom." – Robert Allen

15. "What we really want to do is what we are really meant to do. When we do what we are meant to do, money comes to us, doors open for us, we feel useful, and the work we do feels like play to us." – Julia Cameron

16. "A budget is more than just a series of numbers on a page. It is an embodiment of our values." – Barack Obama

17. "Never spend your money before you have earned it." – Thomas Jefferson

18. "If you would be wealthy, think of saving as well as getting." – Benjamin Franklin

19. "A wise person should have money in their head, but not in their heart." – Jonathan Swift

20. "There is a gigantic difference between earning a great deal of money and being rich." – Marlene Dietrich

21. "Too many people spend money they haven't earned, to buy things they don't want, to impress people they don't like." – Will Rogers

22. "Money is only a tool. It will take you wherever you wish, but it will not replace you as the driver." – Ayn Rand

23. "The habit of saving is itself an education; it fosters every virtue, teaches self-denial, cultivates the sense of order, trains to forethought, and so broadens the mind." – T.T. Munger

24. "There is no dignity quite so impressive, and no independence quite so important, as living within your means." – Calvin Coolidge

25. "Every time you borrow money, you're robbing your future self." – Nathan Morris

26. "Before you speak, listen. Before you write, think. Before you spend, earn. Before you invest, investigate. Before you criticize, wait. Before you pray, forgive. Before you quit, try. Before you retire, save. Before you die, give." – William A. Ward

27. "Don't think money does everything, or you are going to do everything for money." – Voltaire

28. "It's good to have money and the things that money can buy, but it's good, too, to check up once in a while and make sure that you haven't lost the things that money can't buy." – George Lorimer

29. "We make a living by what we get. We make a life by what we give." – Winston Churchill

30. "You can give without loving, but you cannot love without giving." – Amy Carmichael

31. "Don't tell me what you value. Show me your budget, and I'll tell you what you value." – Joe Biden

32. "If you're saving, you're succeeding." – Steve Burkholder

33. "Money does not dictate your lifestyle, It's what you do to get it and how you manage your finances that determines your lifestyle." – Wayne Chirisa

34. "Wealth is not about having a lot of money; it's about having a lot of options." – Chris Rock

35. "People say that money is not the key to happiness, but I always figured if you have enough money, you can have a key made." – Joan Rivers

36. "You can only become truly accomplished at something you love. Don't make money your goal. Instead, pursue the things you love doing, and then do them so well that people can't take their eyes off you." – Maya Angelou

37. "Manage your spending by creating and sticking to a budget." – Alexa Von Tobel

38. "The gratification of wealth is not found in mere possession or in lavish expenditure, but in its wise application." – Miguel de Cervantes

39. "A big part of financial freedom is having your heart and mind free from worry about the what-ifs of life." – Suze Orman

40. "Money isn't as far as it seems, KNOWLEDGE is!" - Sir Unicorn

41. "Learn to "name your money(s) and insist that their names are never changed" - Sir. Unicorn

42. "God never made anyone rich or poor, they made themselves so. The biggest difference between the rich and poor is not the money in their pocket but their mindset." – Apostle Joshua Selman

43. "Anything that does not subscribe to the law of process, run away from it." - Apostle Joshua Selman

44. "Break-through comes instantly, but preparation for that breakthrough takes time." - Apostle Joshua Selman

45. "God gives men to speed, but he does not rush them." - Apostle Joshua Selman

46. "Stop trying to look rich, pay the price and be rich." - Apostle Joshua Selman

47. "Too many people spend money they earned to buy things they don't want..to impress people that they don't like. –Will Roger

48. "A wise person should have money in their head, but not in their heart." –Jonathan Swift

49. "Wealth consists not in having great possessions, but in having few wants." – Epictetus

50. "Money often costs too much." –Ralph Waldo Emerson

51. "Everyday is a bank account, and time is our currency. No one is rich, no one is poor, we've got 24 hours each." –Christopher Rice

52. "It's how you deal with failure that determines how you achieve success." – David Feherty

53. "Frugality includes all the other virtues." – Cicero

54. "I love money. I love everything about it. I bought some pretty good stuff. Got me a

$300 pair of socks. Got a fur sink. An electric dog polisher. A gasoline powered turtleneck sweater. And, of course, I bought some dumb stuff, too." –Steve Martin

55. "An investment in knowledge pays the best interest." –Benjamin Franklin

56. "I will tell you the secret to getting rich on Wall Street. You try to be greedy when others are fearful. And you try to be fearful when others are greedy." –Warren Buffett

57. "Annual income twenty pounds, annual expenditure nineteen six, result happiness. Annual income twenty pounds, annual expenditure twenty pound ought and six, result misery." –Charles Dickens

58. "Opportunity is missed by most people because it is dressed in overalls and looks like work." –Thomas Edison

59. "What we really want to do is what we are really meant to do. When we do what we are meant to do, money comes to us, doors open for us, we feel useful, and the work we do feels like play to us." –Julia Cameron

60. "I never attempt to make money on the stock market. I buy on the assumption that they could close the market the next day and not reopen it for ten years." –Warren Buffet

61. "A nickel ain't worth a dime anymore." –Yogi Berra

62. "Money never made a man happy yet, nor will it. The more a man has, the more he

wants. Instead of filling a vacuum, it makes one." –Benjamin Franklin

63. "Many people take no care of their money till they come nearly to the end of it, and others do just the same with their time." –Johann Wolfgang von Goethe

64. "Formal education will make you a living; self-education will make you a fortune." –Jim Rohn

65. "Money is only a tool. It will take you wherever you wish, but it will not replace you as the driver." –Ayn Rand

66. "Financial peace isn't the acquisition of stuff. It's learning to live on less than you make, so you can give money back and have money to invest. You can't win until you do this." –Dave Ramsey

67. "It is not the man who has too little, but the man who craves more, that is poor." – Seneca

68. "It's not the employer who pays the wages. Employers only handle the money. It's the customer who pays the wages." –Henry Ford

69. "He who loses money, loses much; He who loses a friend, loses much more; He who loses faith, loses all." –Eleanor Roosevelt

70. "Happiness is not in the mere possession of money; it lies in the joy of achievement, in the thrill of creative effort." –Franklin D. Roosevelt

71. "Empty pockets never held anyone back. Only empty heads and empty hearts can do that." –Norman Vincent Peale

72. "It's good to have money and the things that money can buy, but it's good, too, to check up once in a while and make sure that you haven't lost the things that money can't buy." –George Lorimer

73. "You can only become truly accomplished at something you love. Don't make money your goal. Instead, pursue the things you love doing, and then do them so well that people can't take their eyes off you." –Maya Angelou

74. "Buy when everyone else is selling and hold until everyone else is buying. That's not just a catchy slogan. It's the very essence of successful investing." –J. Paul Getty

75. "If money is your hope for independence you will never have it. The only real security that a man will have in this world is a reserve of knowledge, experience, and ability." –Henry Ford

76. "If all the economists were laid end to end, they'd never reach a conclusion." –George Bernard Shaw

77. "How many millionaires do you know who have become wealthy by investing in savings accounts? I rest my case." –Robert G. Allen

78. "I made my money the old-fashioned way. I was very nice to a wealthy relative right before he died." –Malcolm Forbes

79. "Innovation distinguishes between a leader and a follower." –Steve Jobs

80. "The real measure of your wealth is how much you'd be worth if you lost all your money." –Anonymous

81. "Money is a terrible master but an excellent servant." –P.T. Barnum

82. "Try to save something while your salary is small; it's impossible to save after you begin to earn more." –Jack Benny

83. "Wealth is the ability to fully experience life." –Henry David Thoreau

84. "The individual investor should act consistently as an investor and not as a speculator." –Ben Graham

85. "I'm a great believer in luck, and I find the harder I work the more I have of it." – Thomas Jefferson

86. "You must gain control over your money or the lack of it will forever control you." –Dave Ramsey

87. "Investing should be more like watching paint dry or watching grass grow. If you want excitement, take $800 and go to Las Vegas." –Paul Samuelson

88. "Every time you borrow money, you're robbing your future self." –Nathan W. Morris

89. "Rich people have small TVs and big libraries, and poor people have small libraries and big TVs." –Zig Ziglar

90. "Never spend your money before you have it." –Thomas Jefferson

91. "The stock market is filled with individuals who know the price of everything, but the value of nothing." –Phillip Fisher

92. "Wealth is not his that has it, but his that enjoys it." –Benjamin Franklin

93. "It's not how much money you make, but how much money you keep, how hard it works for you, and how many generations you keep it for." –Robert Kiyosaki

94. "I have not failed. I've just found 10,000 ways that won't work." –Thomas A. Edison

95. "If you don't value your time, neither will others. Stop giving away your time and

talents. Value what you know & start charging for it." –Kim Garst

96. "Here's to the crazy ones. The misfits. The rebels. The troublemakers. The round pegs in the square holes. The ones who see things differently. They're not fond of rules. And they have no respect for the status quo. You can quote them, disagree with them, glorify or vilify them. About the only thing you can't do is ignore them. Because they change things. They push the human race forward. And while some may see them as the crazy ones, we see genius. Because the people who are crazy enough to think they can change the world, are the ones who do." –Steve Jobs

97. "The habit of saving is itself an education; it fosters every virtue, teaches self-denial, cultivates the sense of order, trains to forethought, and so broadens the mind." – T.T. Munger

98. "Don't tell me what you value, show me your budget, and I'll tell you what you value." – Joe Biden

99. "If you live for having it all, what you have is never enough." –Vicki Robin

100. "Before you speak, listen. Before you write, think. Before you spend, earn. Before you invest, investigate. Before you criticize, wait. Before you pray, forgive. Before you quit, try. Before you retire, save. Before you die, give." –William A. Ward

101. "We make a living by what we get, but we make a life by what we give." – Winston Churchill

102. "Wealth after all is a relative thing since he that has little and wants less is richer than he that has much and wants more." –Charles Caleb Colton

103. "Not everything that can be counted counts, and not everything that counts can be counted." –Albert Einstein

104. "It is time for us to stand and cheer for the doer, the achiever, the one who recognizes the challenge and does something about it." –Vince Lombardi

105. "It's not the situation, but whether we react (negative) or respond (positive) to the situation that's important." –Zig Ziglar

106. "A successful man is one who can lay a firm foundation with the bricks others have thrown at him." –David Brinkley

107.   "Let him who would enjoy a good future waste none of his present." –Roger Babson

108.   "Courage is being scared to death, but saddling up anyway." –John Wayne

109.   "Live as if you were to die tomorrow. Learn as if you were to live forever." – Mahatma Gandhi

110.   "Twenty years from now you will be more disappointed by the things that you didn't do than by the ones you did do." – Mark Twain

111.   It is our choices, that show what we truly are, far more than our abilities." –J. K Rowling

112. "The successful warrior is the average man, with laser-like focus." –Bruce Lee

113. "Develop success from failures. Discouragement and failure are two of the surest stepping stones to success." –Dale Carnegie

114. "The question isn't who is going to let me; it's who is going to stop me." –Ayn Rand

115. "Don't let the fear of losing be greater than the excitement of winning." –Robert Kiyosaki

116. "You can't connect the dots looking forward; you can only connect them looking backwards. So you have to trust that the

dots will somehow connect in your future. You have to trust in something – your gut, destiny, life, karma, whatever. This approach has never let me down, and it has made all the difference in my life." –Steve Jobs

117. "Let no feeling of discouragement prey upon you, and in the end you are sure to succeed." –Abraham Lincoln

118. "Screw it, Let's do it!" –Richard Branson

119. "If your ship doesn't come in, swim out to meet it!" –Jonathan Winters

120. "People often say that motivation doesn't last. Well, neither does bathing – that's why we recommend it daily." –Zig Ziglar

121. "A real entrepreneur is somebody who has no safety net underneath them." – Henry Kravis

122. "As long as you're going to be thinking anyway, think big." –Donald Trump

123. "The only place where success comes before work is in the dictionary." –Vidal Sassoon

124. "Success is walking from failure to failure with no loss of enthusiasm." –Winston Churchill

125. "Without continual growth and progress, such words as improvement, achievement, and success have no meaning." –Benjamin Franklin

126. "If plan A fails, remember there are 25 more letters." –Chris Guillebeau

127. "Do not go where the path may lead, go instead where there is no path and leave a trail." –Ralph Waldo Emerson

128. "A journey of a thousand miles must begin with a single step." –Lao Tzu

129. "Do the one thing you think you cannot do. Fail at it. Try again. Do better the second time. The only people who never tumble are those who never mount the high wire. This is your moment. Own it." –Oprah Winfrey

130. "Believe you can and you're halfway there." –Theodore Roosevelt

131. "The Stock Market is designed to transfer money from the Active to the Patient." –Warren Buffett

132. "I'm only rich because I know when I'm wrong…I basically have survived by recognizing my mistakes." –George Soros

133. "Persist – don't take no for an answer. If you're happy to sit at your desk and not take any risk, you'll be sitting at your desk for the next 20 years." –David Rubenstein

134. "If you took our top fifteen decisions out, we'd have a pretty average record. It wasn't hyperactivity, but a hell of a lot of patience. You stuck to your principles and when opportunities came along, you pounced on them with vigor." –Charlie Munger

135. "When buying shares, ask yourself, would you buy the whole company?" –Rene Rivkin

136. "If you have trouble imagining a 20% loss in the stock market, you shouldn't be in stocks." –John Bogle

137. "My old father used to have a saying: If you make a bad bargain, hug it all the tighter." –Abraham Lincoln

138. "It takes as much energy to wish as it does to plan." –Eleanor Roosevelt

139. "The four most expensive words in the English language are, 'This time it's different." –Sir John Templeton

140. "I'd like to live as a poor man with lots of money." –Pablo Picasso

141. "Fortune sides with him who dares." –Virgil

142. "Wealth is like sea-water; the more we drink, the thirstier we become; and the same is true of fame." –Arthur Schopenhauer

143. "If we command our wealth, we shall be rich and free. If our wealth commands us, we are poor indeed." –Edmund Burke

144. "No wealth can ever make a bad man at peace with himself." –Plato

145. "My formula for success is rise early, work late and strike oil." –JP Getty

146. "Robert Kiyosaki Financial Freedom" Quotes

147. "Financial freedom is mental, emotional, and education process." - Suze Orman

148. "More important than how we achieve financial freedom is the why. Find your reasons why you want to be free and wealthy." - Suze Orman

149. "To obtain financial freedom, one must be either a business owner, an investor or both, generating passive income, particularly on a monthly basis." - Suze Orman

150. "Financial freedom is available to those who learn about it and work for it." - Suze Orman

151. "Financial freedom is freedom from fear." - Suze Orman

152. "Financial independence is about having more choices." - Suze Orman

153. If you want to be financially free, you need to become a different person than you are today and let go of whatever has held you back in the past." - Suze Orman

154. "The philosophy of the rich and the poor is this: the rich invest their money and spend what is left. The poor spend their money and invest what is left." - Suze Orman

155. "The key to financial freedom and great wealth is a person's ability or skill to convert earned income into passive income and/or portfolio income." - Suze Orman

156. "When you understand that your self-worth is not determined by your net-worth, then you'll have financial freedom." - Dave Ramsey

157. "A big part of financial freedom is having your heart and mind free from worry about the what-ifs of life." - Dave Ramsey

158. "Financial peace isn't the acquisition of stuff. It's learning to live on less than you make, so you can give money back and have money to invest. You can't win until you do this." - Jim Rohn

159. "You must gain control over your money or the lack of it will forever control you." - Jim Rohn

160. "I believe that through knowledge and discipline, financial peace is possible for all of us." - Jim Rohn

161. "If you will make the sacrifices now that most people aren't willing to make, later on you will be able to live as those folks will never be able to live." - Jim Rohn

162. "To become financially independent, you must turn part of your income into capital; turn capital into enterprise; turn enterprise into profit; turn a profit into an investment, and turn the investment into financial independence." - Jim Rohn

163. "Formal education will make you a living; self-education will make you a fortune." - Jim Rohn

164. "To become financially independent you must turn part of your income into capital; turn capital into enterprise; turn enterprise into profit; turn profit into investment, and turn investment into financial independence." - Jim Rohn

165. "If you are not financially independent by the time you are forty or fifty, it doesn't mean that you are living in the wrong country or at the wrong time. It simply means that you have the wrong plan." - Jim Rohn

166. "Pursuing your passion is fulfilling and leads to financial freedom" – Robert G. Allen

167. "Financial freedom is the power to produce wealth and not necessarily having wealth."– Stephen Covey

168. "Your economic security does not lie in your job; it lies in your own power to produce – to think, to learn, to create, to adapt. That's true financial independence. It's not having wealth; it's having the power to produce wealth." – Stephen Covey

169. "Real wealth is not about money. Real wealth is: not having to go to meetings, not having to spend time with jerks, not being locked into status games, not feeling like you have to say 'yes,' not worrying about others claiming your time and energy. Real wealth is about freedom." – James Clear

170. "Working because you want to and not because you have to is financial freedom."– Tony Robbins

171. "You either master money, or, on some level, money masters you." – Tony Robbins

172. "The secret to wealth is simple: Find a way to do more for others than anyone else does. Become more valuable. Do more. Give more. Be more. Serve more." – Tony Robbins

173. "Money is a terrible master but an excellent servant." – PT Barnum

174. "Financial fitness is not a pipe dream or a state of mind. It's a reality if you are willing to pursue it and embrace it." – Will Robinson

175. "Rich people believe 'I create my life.' Poor people believe 'Life happens to me.'" – T. Harv Eker

176. "My definition of financial freedom is simple: it is the ability to live the lifestyle you desire without having to work or rely on anyone else for money." – T. Harv Eker

177. "To get rich, you have to be making money while you're asleep." – David Bailey

178. "Wealth is the ability to fully experience life." -Henry David Thoreau

179. "At least eighty percent of millionaires are self-made. That is, they started with nothing but ambition and energy, the same way most of us start." – Brian Tracy

180. "Money is something we choose to trade our life energy for." – Vicki Robin

181. "The goal isn't more money. The goal is living life on your terms." – Chris Brogan

182. "I don't believe in spending money lavishly, now that I'm making money." – Ansel Elgort

183. "If you're saving, you're succeeding." – Steve Burkholder

184. "Financial planning and discipline is key to one's financial freedom." – Kishorkumar Balpalli

185. "Millions wish for financial freedom, but only those that make it a priority have millions." – Oscar Auliq-Ice

186. "Whenever you find yourself on the side of the majority, it is time to pause and reflect." – Mark Twain

187. "The speed of your success is limited only by your dedication and what you're willing to sacrifice." – Nathan W. Morris

188. "Every time you borrow money, you're robbing your future self." – Nathan W. Morris

189. "Financial security and independence are like a three-legged stool resting on savings, insurance, and investments." – Brian Tracy

190. "The habit of saving is itself an education; it fosters every virtue, teaches

self-denial, cultivates the sense of order, trains to forethought, and so broadens the mind." – T.T. Munger

191. "The goal is to retire young and financially free"- Philip Michael

192. "You become rich in your mind long before you become rich in your bank account"- Philip Michael

193. "Hustle like you have no friends. Grind like nobody has your back"- Philip Michael

194. "if you can still count your money, work harder"- Philip Michael

195. "You are your own driver to financial freedom"- Sir. Unicorn

196. "Do all the stress you can to rest all the rest you need"- Sir. Unicorn

197. "If it is about making money, I am in"- Sir. Unicorn

198. "Learn to be attractive to wealth"- Sir. Unicorn

199. "Don't remain where men put you"- Pastor Emmanuel Okonkwo

200. "Jesus will help you, just work harder and keep grinding"- Sir. Unicorn.

CONCLUSSION

www.ingramcontent.com/pod-product-compliance
Lightning Source LLC
Chambersburg PA
CBHW050316220526
45465CB00005B/2018